Contents

Toys

Monica Hughes

Heinemann
LIBRARY

Little Nippers

www.heinemann.co.uk/library
Visit our website to find out more information about **Heinemann Library** books.

To order:
☎ Phone 44 (0) 1865 888066
🖹 Send a fax to 44 (0) 1865 314091
🖳 Visit the Heinemann Bookshop at www.heinemann.co.uk/library to browse our
catalogue and order online.

First published in Great Britain by Heinemann
Library, Halley Court, Jordan Hill, Oxford
OX2 8EJ, part of Harcourt Education.
Heinemann is a registered trademark of Harcourt
Education Ltd.

© Harcourt Education Ltd 2003
The moral right of the proprietor has
been asserted.

Editorial: Sarah Eason and Georga Godwin
Design: Jo Hinton-Malivoire and Tokay,
  Bicester, UK (www.tokay.co.uk)
Picture Research: Rosie Garai and
  Debra Weatherley
Production: Edward Moore

Originated by Dot Gradations Ltd
Printed and bound in China by South China
Printing Company

ISBN 0 431 18642 1 (hardback)
07 06 05 04 03
10 9 8 7 6 5 4 3 2 1

ISBN 0 431 18647 2 (paperback)
07 06 05 04 03
10 9 8 7 6 5 4 3 2 1

British Library Cataloguing in Publication Data
Hughes, Monica
Now and Then – Toys
790.1'33'09
A full catalogue record for this book is available
from the British Library.

Acknowledgements
The Publishers would like to thank the following
for permission to reproduce photographs:
Bubbles/Jennie Woodcock **p. 16**; Bubbles/Denise
Wills **p. 8**; Corbis/Bettman **p. 23**; Corbis/David
Katzenstein **p. 18**; Corbis/Roy Morsch **p. 6**; Getty
Images/Frank Siteman **p. 12**; Getty Images/
Hulton Archive **pp. 5**, **7**, **9**, **11**, **15**, **19**; Index
Stock Imagery **p. 14**; Mary Evans Picture Library
p. 17; Popperfoto **p. 21**; Popperfoto/CPL **p. 13**;
Steve Behr **pp. 4**, **22**; Topham **p. 10**; Trip/H.
Rogers **p. 20**.

Cover photograph reproduced with permission
of Getty Images/Hulton Archive.

The Publishers would like to thank Annie Davy
for her assistance in the preparation of this book.

Every effort has been made to contact copyright
holders of any material reproduced in this book.
Any omissions will be rectified in subsequent
printings if notice is given to the Publishers.

5

Scooters

Now scooters are **light** and **fast**.

Whoosh!

6

A scooter for three was **fun** to play with.

Then

Prams

It is **fun** to push a buggy or a pram.

Now

Then

Look how prams have changed.

9

Then

Games

A computer game is **exciting** to play with a friend.

Now

12

Trains

Now

Children have always loved train sets. Do you have one?

Then

15

Construction toys

Now

These bricks fit together very easily.

Click!

16

Then

This set looks much more difficult.

Moving toys

Now

Vrooom!

This remote controlled car goes very **fast**.

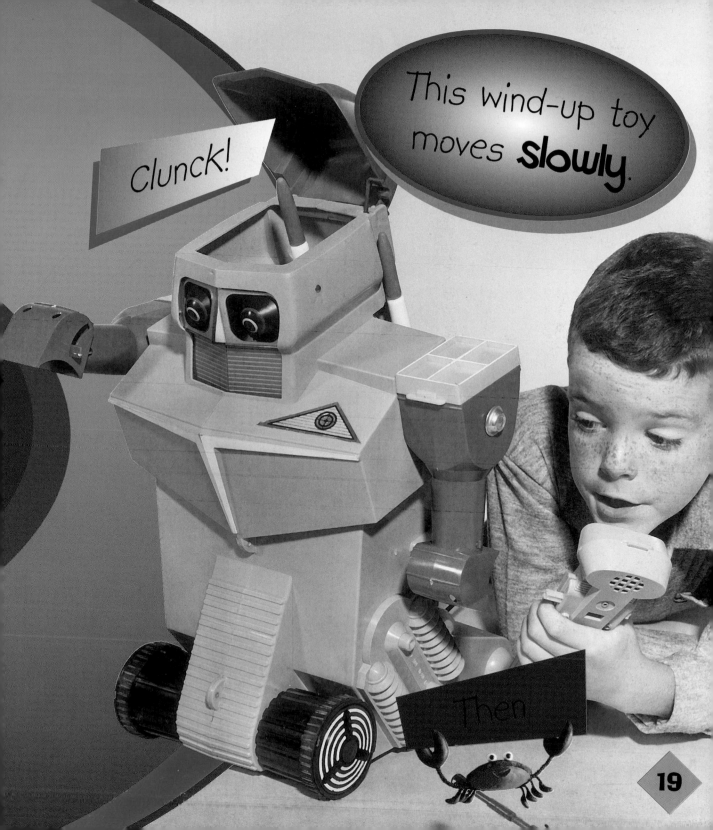

Soft toys

Look at all these soft toys.
Have you got a favourite?

Then

Marbles

Now we have a **super** marble run.

Then

These children also enjoyed playing with marbles.

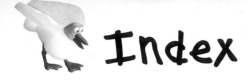

Index

The end

Notes for adults

This series supports the child's knowledge and understanding of their world, in particular their personal, social and emotional development. The following Early Learning Goals are relevant to the series:

- make connections between different parts of their life experience
- show an awareness of change
- begin to differentiate between past and present
- introduce language that enables them to talk about their experiences in greater depth and detail.

It is important to relate the **Now** photographs to the child's own experiences and so help them differentiate between the past and present. The **Then** photographs can be introduced by using phrases like: *When I was your age, When granddad was a boy, Before you were born.* By comparing the two photographs they can begin to identify similarities and differences between the present and the past. Ask open-ended questions like: Do you remember when . . ? What might it be like . . ? What do you think . . ? This will help the child to develop their own ideas and extend their thinking.

Many of the basic toys shown in the **Then** photographs will be familiar to the child. There may be changes to the type of materials used, for example plastic **Now** compared with metal **Then**, but many of the same toys have been enjoyed by children for several years. The child might suggest why they think this might be – relating it to their own favourite toys. Some things have changed especially in relation to computer games and electronic toys.

A follow up activity could include a visit to a museum to see real examples of toys from different periods. You could describe your own favourite childhood toys and the child could identify their own, and give reasons for their choice.